DATAWORLD

MICROCHIP MAGIC

ROBIN KERROD

GRAFTON BOOKS
A Division of the Collins Publishing Group

LONDON GLASGOW
TORONTO SYDNEY AUCKLAND

Grafton Books
A Division of the Collins Publishing Group
8 Grafton Street, London W1X 3LA

Published by Grafton Books 1986

Copyright © Lionheart Books 1986

British Library Cataloguing in Publication Data

Kerrod, Robin
  Microchip magic.— (Dataworld; V.1)
  1. Digital communications — Juvenile literature
  I. Title   II. Series
  621.38'0413   TK5103.7

  ISBN 0-246-12710-4

This book was conceived, edited and produced by
Lionheart Books
10 Chelmsford Square
London NW10 3AR

Editor Lionel Bender
Designer Malcolm Smythe
Picture Researcher Dee Robinson
Editorial Assistant Madeleine Bender
Illustrator Rob Shone
Typeset by Dorchester Typesetting Group Ltd.

Printed and bound in Italy by
New Interlitho, Milan

Contents

The Mighty Micro

Computers were only recently invented, but you'll find them everywhere. They are used to control all kinds of machines, from washing machines to factory robots. They help predict the weather, restock supermarket shelves, run bank accounts, help aeroplanes to land safely and guide space probes to distant planets. Some computers are used to print letters, others to sort out envelopes by their postcodes and check the stamps. A powerful computer could do all these at the same time, and still beat you at chess!

Computers hold the key to our modern age, and in particular to information technology, the subject of this series of books. Computers are able to store, process and communicate information much faster than any other machine or human being. Computers appear to be so clever that they are sometimes called electronic brains. However, as yet they are not intelligent in the human sense. They can only do what they are instructed, or programmed, to do. Their great advantage over human brains is that they can carry out calculations at a phenomenal speed. Some can perform several hundred million calculations *every second!*

The home computer
Such superfast computers are used by large government and business organizations. But you no longer have to be a large company to enjoy the advantages computers have to offer. With a home computer you can become your own computer expert. Home computers are referred to as microcomputers because of their small size; most are no bigger than a portable typewriter.

Everything about the micro is minute, including its 'brain', which is incorporated in a wafer-thin crystal no bigger than your fingernail. This tiny wafer is a silicon chip, one of the most remarkable products of the electronic age. You now find it not only in computers but in many other devices as well, from digital watches and pocket calculators to electronic typewriters and even washing machines.

Under the microscope the electronic circuits on a silicon chip show up clearly. This is a memory chip.

Electrons and Chips

Like radios and TV sets, computers work electronically. This means they contain devices that manipulate streams of electrons. Electrons are some of the tiny particles found in the atoms that make up all matter. Under suitable conditions, electrons will flow, and it is a flow of electrons that makes up an electric current.

The electronic devices that allow the computer to carry out its tasks change the direction and strength of electric currents passing through complicated paths, or circuits. Four main kinds of device are used. These are known as resistors, capacitors, diodes and transistors. Resistors are so called because they hold back, or resist, the flow of current. Capacitors are able to store electricity. Diodes act as one-way

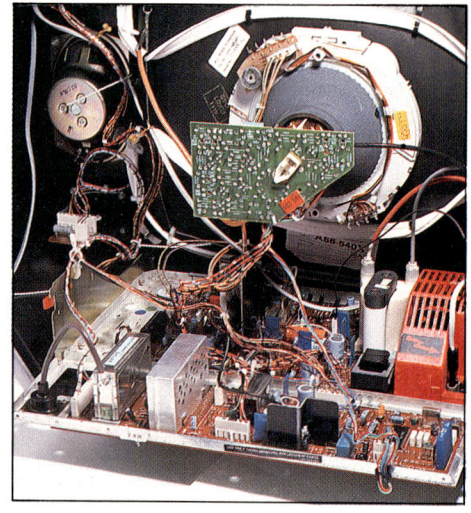

Printed circuit boards are also used in ordinary electronic equipment, such as this TV set, but wires still abound.

switches. Transistors can also act as switches or they can amplify (strengthen) current passing through them.

All these electronic devices can be made from certain kinds of crystal, particularly crystals of silicon. Silicon is one of the commonest chemical elements. It is found in minerals such as sand and clay.

The inside of the Sinclair Spectrum computer, showing details of the electronic circuits. The various components, such as resistors, capacitors and chips, are linked together by connections on a printed circuit board. The most complicated circuitry is microscopic, in the chips.

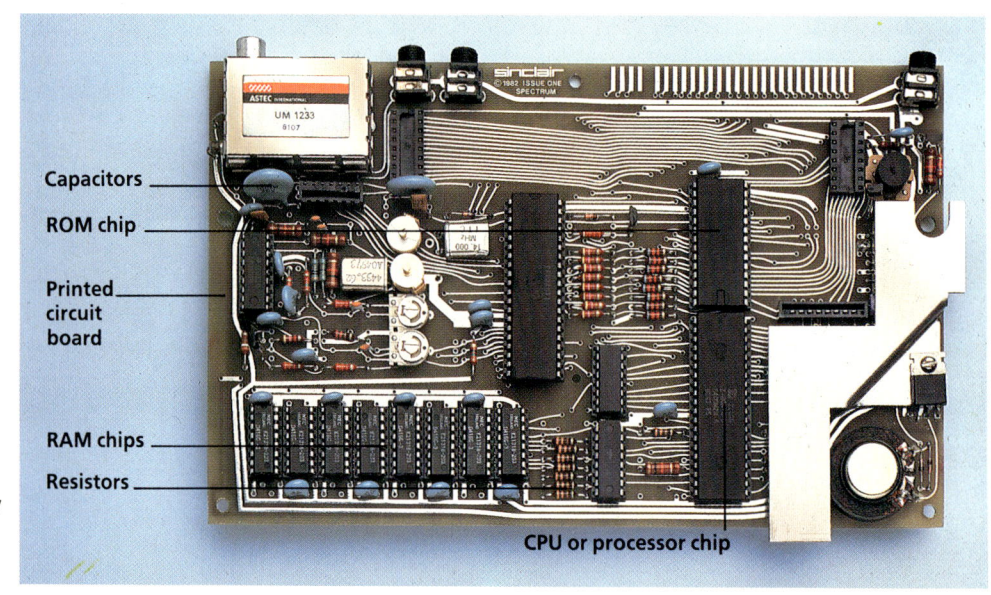

Capacitors

ROM chip

Printed circuit board

RAM chips

Resistors

CPU or processor chip

Integrated circuits

When silicon devices first came into use, they were used separately in electronic circuits. In other words circuits were built up with, say, diodes and transistors connected together by wires. Many radio and TV sets still have this kind of circuit. In computers, however, whole circuits are built up within single silicon crystals. They are called integrated circuits (ICs).

The astonishing thing about integrated circuits is that they can be made unbelievably small. Thousands of circuits can be incorporated in a thin wafer of silicon only about 7 millimetres square. And these circuits may include tens of thousands of individual diodes, transistors, and so on, each smaller than a pinprick.

These wafers are generally called silicon chips. Although they are very complicated devices, they can be mass-produced quite easily. Therefore they are cheap. Thanks to them, we can all be part of the computer revolution.

This advanced silicon chip is smaller than a postage stamp, yet it contains some 200,000 electronic components.

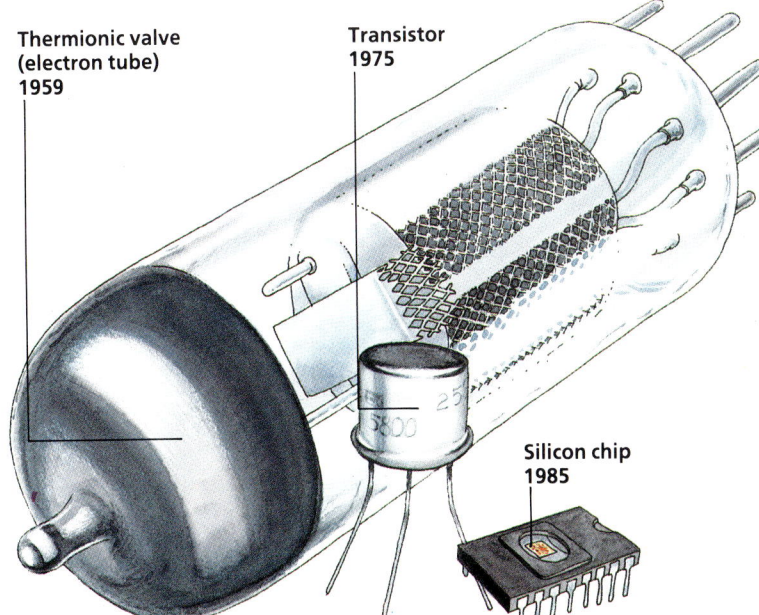

Thermionic valve (electron tube) 1959

Transistor 1975

Silicon chip 1985

Until the 1960s all electronic equipment – radios, TVs, record players and the like – used valves in their circuits. Valves were evacuated glass bulbs containing thin metal plates and grids. They were fragile, consumed a lot of power, and gave out a lot of heat. By the 1970s they had been almost entirely replaced by transistors only a fraction of their size. In the 1980s chips many times smaller still could hold whole electronic circuits containing thousands of transistors and other components.

Chip-Making

Right: The final stage in chip production. The chip has been fixed on to a mount, and fine gold wires lead from it to external contact pins.

It takes a long time to produce a new silicon chip. The first stage is to design the electronic circuits that it will carry. This is the most skilled and time-consuming stage of production. After the electronic circuitry has been finalized, designers work out how to incorporate it into a chip. The method they use is to build up all the various components in the circuit together layer by layer.

A typical transistor consists of three layers of silicon. Each layer has to be specially treated, or doped, so that it is electrically different from the ones above and below it. Then it can function as a switch or an amplifier in an appropriate circuit.

Step by step, layer by layer

The standard method of doping the various layers of silicon is also time-consuming. It involves up to 12 separate stages of masking, coating, exposure to light, etching with acid, and treatment with chemical vapours. A different mask is needed for each layer to ensure that the chemical vapours, the dopants, reach only certain parts of the silicon each time. When all the electronic layers have been built up, a final sequence of masking, etching and vapour treatment takes place that deposits a thin film of aluminium on certain areas. This forms the connections between the components.

In practice, hundreds of chips are made at the same time on circular slices of silicon between 7.5 and 10 centimetres in diameter. Afterwards a computer-controlled probe automatically tests each chip and marks those that are defective.

Finally the silicon disc is sliced by a diamond cutter into individual chips. Each usable chip is mounted on an insulated base, and gold wires connected between it and pins on the base. It is now ready to be fitted into a larger circuit board.

A stage in the production of the mask for one layer of a chip. The circuit layout is about to be reduced in size photographically.

Many different masks are used in sequence to form layers in the silicon. The regions to be doped are masked (shown dark in the pictures).

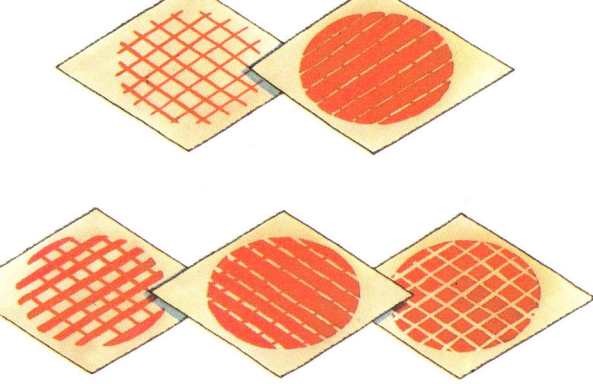

Oxide layer

Silicon

Window

Above left: Silicon slices ready to go into the furnace for doping with chemicals.

Above: Examining the finished chips, still connected together on the slice.

In chip manufacture, the silicon is first oxidized. By masking, windows are opened up in the oxide layer, through which dopant diffuses into the silicon.

Calculators and Watches

The most widespread use of silicon chips is in pocket calculators and digital watches. Hundreds of different kinds of pocket calculator are now available. They are distinguishable by their different functions – the things they can do. Calculators are simple computers that can carry out a fixed and limited set of instructions. They perform calculations in the same way as a proper computer, working with binary numbers (see page 18). They are pocket-sized because they need just a tiny battery to power them. Some need no battery at all, being powered by solar cells.

The simplest calculators, costing only a few pounds, are able to do only the most basic calculations – addition, subtraction, multiplication and division. Some of them are little bigger than a credit card. Other calculators incorporate a clock and calendar, and one or more alarms. They may even play music or games of some sort.

The most advanced scientific calculators have many extra functions, such as squares, square roots, logarithms, sines, tangents, a memory and so on. The top-of-the-range models are programmable. This means that you can feed your own instructions into them, just as you can into a proper computer.

Digits on display
Calculators show the numbers they are working with, and the results, in a display window. Usually there is a

Thanks to the versatile silicon chip, calculator watches like this are possible. It also features a memory, for use during computations, and stop-watch and alarm functions.

This pocket calculator also boasts a variety of functions. In various modes it can act as a boxing game, clock or calculator.

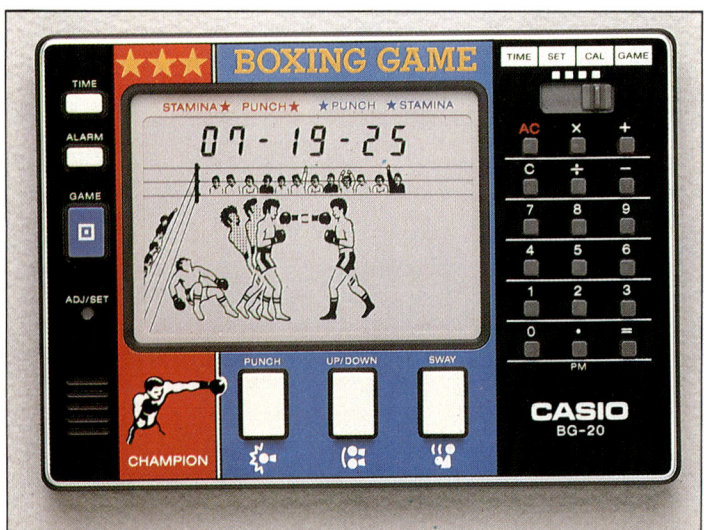

liquid crystal display (LCD) of black on white. Liquid crystals are ingenious materials that twist the path of light passing through them. When electricity is applied to them, they untwist the light path. This effect is used to allow light to be reflected through the display (white) or block it (black). Numbers are formed when the light is blocked.

Digital watches have this kind of display too. They are so called because they show the time in digits (numbers). Like all clocks, the digital watch measures time by means of a regulator, a device that controls the speed of a certain process. The watch uses the vibrations of a wafer-thin crystal of quartz. The electronic circuits in the watch's chip count the vibrations into seconds, minutes, hours and so on. They then send signals to the display, which shows the time.

Chip technology has made possible the quartz digital watch, which shows the time by numbers (digits). This picture, though, shows a quartz analogue watch, in which the circuits on the chip (top) control the movement of conventional hands.

Chips and calculators
The keyboard and circuitry of a simple pocket calculator. It has keys for each number from 0-9, and for the various arithmetic functions (+, −, ×, ÷). The display is by LED light-emitting diodes.

Plastic casing

Display window

Keys

LED display

On/off switch

Connections to LED display

Chip mount

Resistors

Capacitors

Circuit connections

The inside view of the calculator shows various components in place on a printed circuit board. The calculator's 'brain' is a chip mounted within the larger black block.

Computer Basics

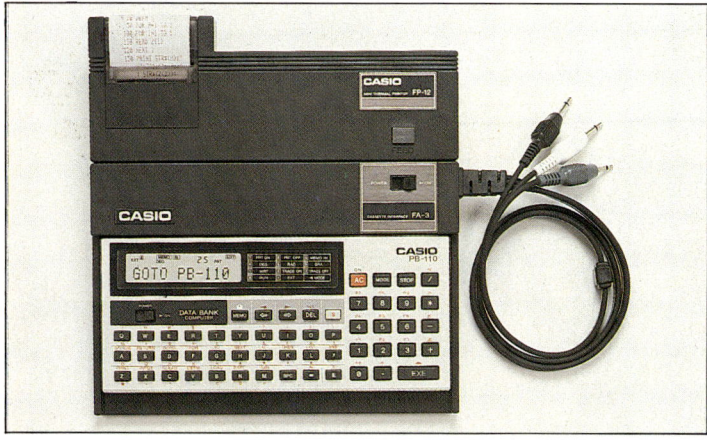

A pocket-sized computer, with plug-in printer attached.

Working with a popular home computer, the Spectrum.

A small mainframe computer, with large memory store.

Today the computer we are most familiar with is the digital computer. It is referred to as digital because it handles instructions and information in the form of individual numbers, or digits. There is another type of computer called an analogue computer. Such computers work by measuring constantly changing values like an ordinary watch measures time. They are used for special purposes, mostly in science and engineering.

A brief history

The first digital computers were built in the 1940s. They were huge machines that filled a large room. The room had to be air-conditioned because the electronic components used in their circuits produced a great deal of heat. In the 1960s much smaller computers made with transistors came into use. And computers have been getting smaller ever since. Thanks to the minuscule silicon chip, the latest typewriter-sized computers have incredible computing power, as much as a room-sized computer of 20 years ago.

Three kinds of digital computer are generally recognized, distinguished by their size and computing power. At the bottom of the range is the microcomputer, which is the kind generally used in the home. Next comes the minicomputer, widely used in business, which can perform many more tasks and has a greater capacity to store and process information. At the top of the range is the mainframe computer. This has a vast capacity for information processing and storage and can carry out many functions at the same time. It is used by large companies, government departments, colleges and universities.

The parts of a computer system
All these computers work in much the same way and are made up of similar kinds of electronic equipment. The pieces of equipment that make up a computer are collectively called the hardware. The set of instructions that must be fed into a computer to make it perform a particular job is called the program. Different programs for a computer together form what is known as the software. The unprocessed information a computer handles is called the data. Computers are in fact often referred to as data processors.

The heart of a computer is the central processing unit, or CPU. This controls the whole computer and carries out all calculations and operations. It acts upon instructions fed into it in the program. And when required for processing, it calls up data stored in a memory unit. Various devices are used to feed programs and data into the computer and extract data from the computer. They are known as input and output devices. In the following pages we shall investigate computer hardware and software in a little more detail.

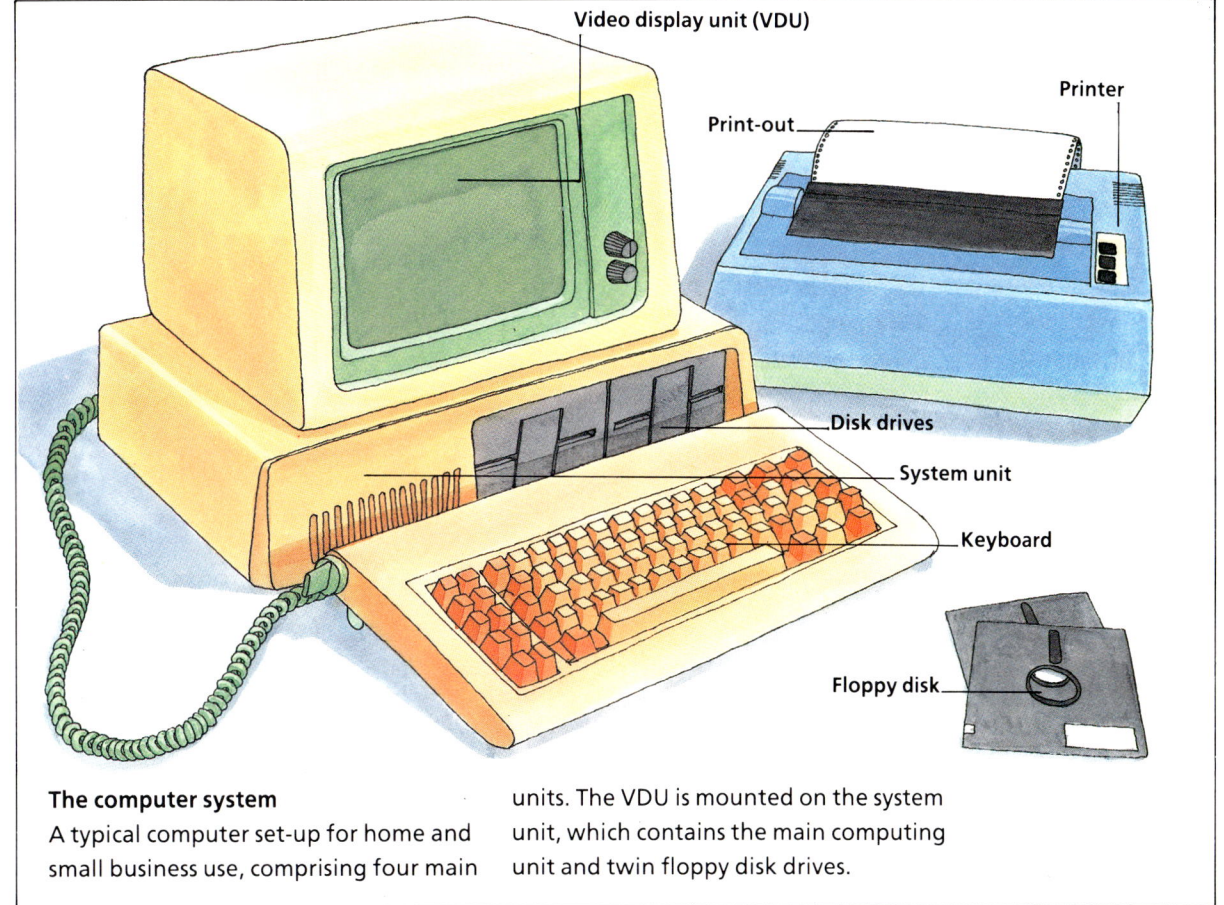

Video display unit (VDU)

Printer

Print-out

Disk drives

System unit

Keyboard

Floppy disk

The computer system
A typical computer set-up for home and small business use, comprising four main units. The VDU is mounted on the system unit, which contains the main computing unit and twin floppy disk drives.

Bits, Bytes, ROMs and RAMs

When we humans do sums (make calculations), we generally use decimal numbers. We use the ten digits from 0 to 9. And we build up larger units of tens, hundreds and thousands by putting the numbers in different places. The number 2345 means two thousand ($2 \times 10 \times 10 \times 10$), three hundred ($3 \times 10 \times 10$) and forty ($4 \times 10$)-five ($5 \times 1$). In other words, in the decimal number system place values from right to left go up in multiples of 10.

The decimal number system is far too complicated for a computer to use for its calculations. It uses instead the much simpler binary number system. This is based upon just two digits, 0 and 1. Computers can work readily with these two binary digits, or bits, because their circuits can easily recognize two states, the flow (1) and non-flow (0) of electric current.

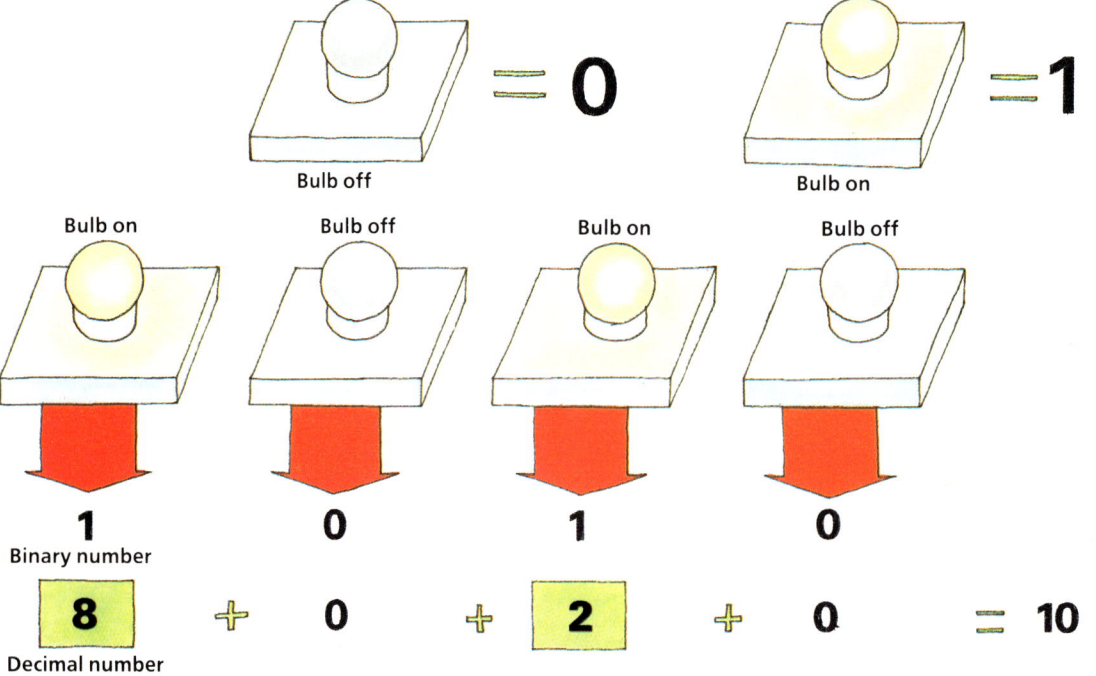

Decimal value	8	0	2	0
Binary digit	1	0	1	0
Pulse				
Voltage				

Binary numbers and codes

In electric circuits, we can represent the two states of the binary code as the flow (1) and non-flow (0) of electricity, and depict them by light bulbs that are lit (1) and unlit (0). All ordinary decimal numbers can be represented in binary code, with place values going up in powers of 2 from right to left (see table). The number decimal 10 is represented in binary code as 1010, which we can illustrate by means of lighted bulbs as above. In the computer, the number is represented by a pattern of electrical pulses.

Working with binary numbers

All data and instructions fed into the computer must be translated into binary number code. Only then can the computer 'understand' and use them. Fortunately, the computer does this translation itself (see page 20). Most microcomputers handle data, information and so on, as sets of eight-bit units, which are called bytes. Mini- and mainframe computers tend to use 16- and 32-bit units.

The computer stores all the coded information fed into it in its memory, or rather memories. It has two kinds of memory. The read-only memory (ROM) is a permanent memory. It contains the essential information the computer needs in order just to work. The random-access memory (RAM) is a temporary memory. It holds the instructions and data the computer needs to perform a particular task. The power of a computer is often expressed in terms of the size of its RAM. A typical home computer has a RAM of over 64,000 bytes.

Different types of code

Many everyday goods and items carry digitally coded information which can be fed directly to computers.

It is expensive and time-consuming for chip manufacturers to design and produce chips custom-made for every requirement. Often, therefore, they start with a chip of standard circuits, a so-called uncommitted chip (far left). Then they connect up the circuits in whatever way a customer wishes (left).

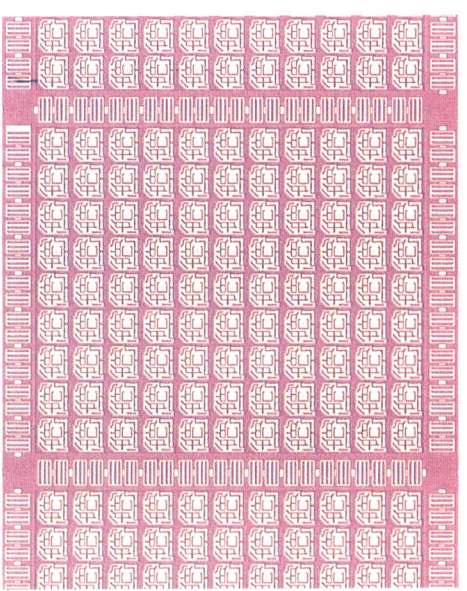

Programming

Before we can make a computer do anything useful, we must program it. We have to feed it with, or input, a program, which is a set of instructions that tells it what to do with the information we will supply.

As we have seen, computers can only handle information in the form of binary code. We can instruct the computer directly in binary code, but this is very laborious and impractical for ordinary computer users. Usually we instruct a computer in a special language that

it can recognize. Then the computer itself translates this language into binary and its own machine code.

Computer languages use a simplified form of English, rather like a kind of shorthand. Several languages are in use for general and special applications. The language most widely used by home computer users is appropriately called BASIC. In science, a language called FORTRAN (short for Formula Translation) is widely used. Business users often use the language COBOL (Common Business Orientated Language). These languages use different command words and symbols for the various computer operations.

Here are excerpts from three programs written in different computer languages. The LOGO program gives instructions for a 'Turtle' robot. The AML program controls an assembly robot. The BASIC program is for the conversion of temperature scales.

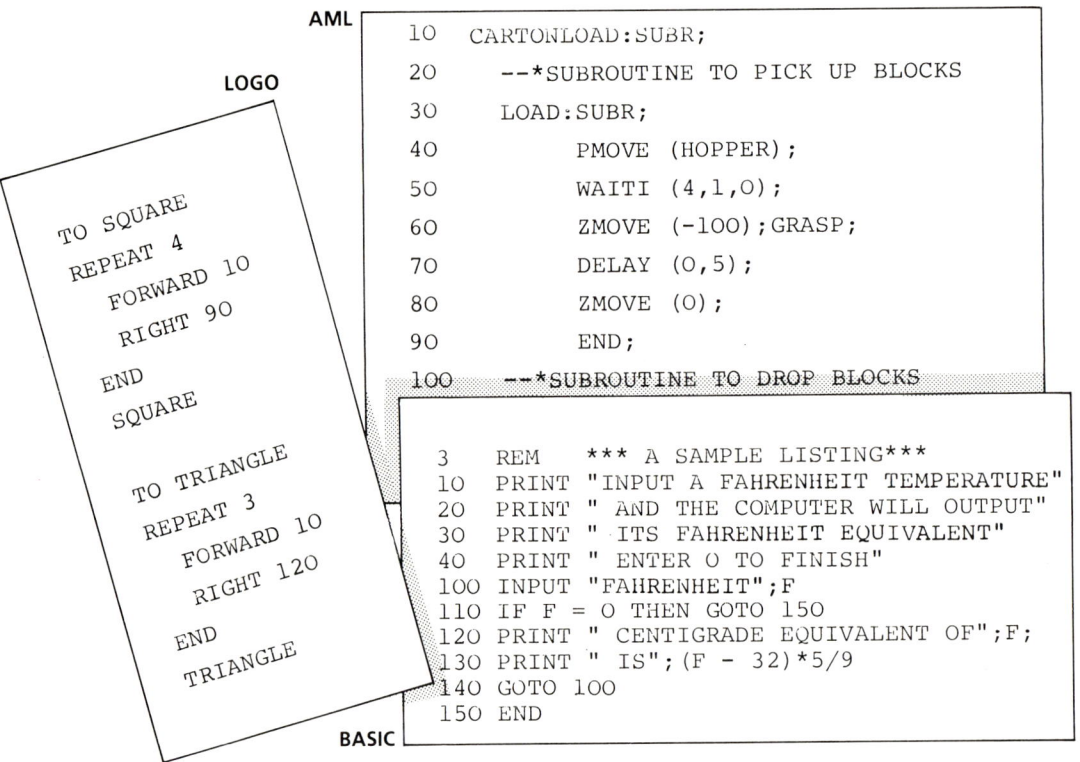

AML
```
10    CARTONLOAD:SUBR;
20      --*SUBROUTINE TO PICK UP BLOCKS
30      LOAD:SUBR;
40          PMOVE (HOPPER);
50          WAITI (4,1,0);
60          ZMOVE (-100);GRASP;
70          DELAY (0,5);
80          ZMOVE (0);
90          END;
100     --*SUBROUTINE TO DROP BLOCKS
```

LOGO
```
TO SQUARE
REPEAT 4
   FORWARD 10
   RIGHT 90
END
SQUARE

TO TRIANGLE
REPEAT 3
   FORWARD 10
   RIGHT 120
END
TRIANGLE
```

BASIC
```
3    REM    *** A SAMPLE LISTING***
10   PRINT "INPUT A FAHRENHEIT TEMPERATURE"
20   PRINT " AND THE COMPUTER WILL OUTPUT"
30   PRINT " ITS FAHRENHEIT EQUIVALENT"
40   PRINT " ENTER 0 TO FINISH"
100  INPUT "FAHRENHEIT";F
110  IF F = 0 THEN GOTO 150
120  PRINT " CENTIGRADE EQUIVALENT OF";F;
130  PRINT " IS";(F - 32)*5/9
140  GOTO 100
150  END
```

Using computer language

In BASIC many of the command words used have an obvious meaning: PRINT prints out (outputs) something you specify; RUN sets in progress the program you have fed into the computer; GOTO directs you to another part of the program; LIST displays the program line by line; and CLS clears the screen.

Writing a program is quite a lengthy process because the instructions to the computer must be given in a series of very simple steps. It is usually helpful before starting the program to draw a diagram showing each of these steps, and the order in which they must go. Such a diagram is called a flowchart.

When you first start program writing, you will probably make some mistakes, and the program won't work. We say there are bugs in it. Often, though, the computer will show you where the mistakes occur by printing a message such as 'BAD LINE' or '?I/O ERROR' on the screen.

Flowcharts

It is useful before writing a program to draw a flowchart, setting out the step-by-step sequence that the program must follow. This is a flowchart for a program we could call 'Odds and Evens'. It shows the steps that must be taken to determine whether a number is odd or even.

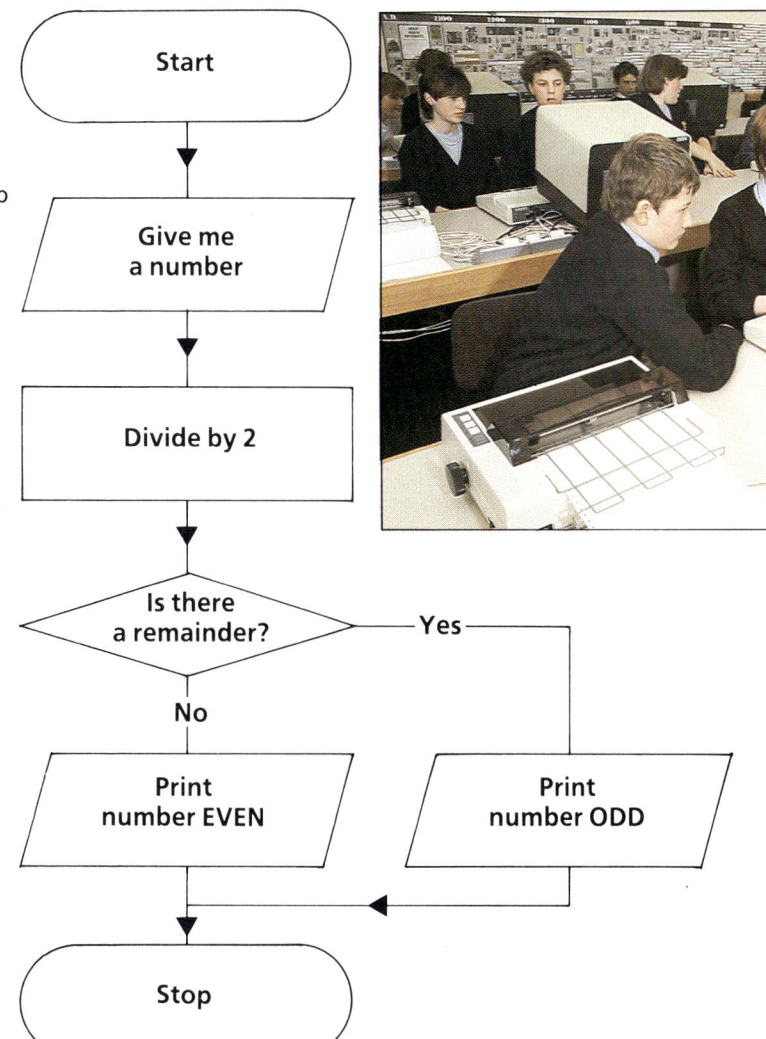

A computer class at a secondary school. Pupils are now taught basic programming skills at an early age. Many also carry on computing at home on the increasingly popular microcomputers.

21

Input/Output

You can input instructions and data into a computer in a variety of ways. Most commonly you communicate with a computer by means of a keyboard, rather like a typewriter keyboard. The keyboard is one example of an input device. It is usually linked with a visual display unit (VDU). When you type instructions on the keyboard, the words appear on the VDU screen.

When writing and using your own programs, you enter them into the computer via the keyboard. For future use you can store, or save, the programs by recording them on magnetic tapes or disks. Thereafter you can feed the programs back into the computer from the tapes or disks. So you have two other methods of input.

For most home computers you can use an ordinary cassette tape recorder and ordinary magnetic tape to save programs. But some computers require a special tape recorder. Others have built-in miniature recorders, or microdrives, for storage.

Floppy and hard disks, printers and plotters

The magnetic disks used for program and data storage are of two types. Most common are the floppy disks, so called because they are soft and flexible. They are placed in disk drive units which hold them in the centre and spin them round rather like a record but at considerably faster speeds. Information is fed to or taken from them by a kind of pick-up called a read/write head.

A selection of input/output hardware for the Apple Macintosh computer. From left to right, this includes a modem, for sending signals via the telephone lines; a high-speed printer; a rolling 'mouse'; keyboard connected with the combined processor and VDU; an additional disk drive; and a numeric keypad for lengthy figure work.

'Floppies' are removed from the disk drive after use. The other kind of computer magnetic disk, however, is permanently enclosed. Known as the Winchester, it is a hard disk with a large storage capacity.

The results, or output, of the computing operations can be displayed on the VDU or recorded tape or disk. A permanent visible record, or hard copy, can be provided by a printer or plotter. Two kinds of printer are commonly used. Dot-matrix printers build up characters (letters, figures, symbols) from a pattern of dots. Daisy-wheel printers print out proper characters like a typewriter. The high-speed printer of mainframe computers can print up to 2000 lines a minute, with each line 120 characters long. A plotter uses one or more pens – coloured if desirable – to draw diagrams and charts.

Data and programs are fed into the Sinclair QL 128K computer by means of microdrive cartridges, which contain spools of miniature magnetic tape. The QL has two built-in microdrives.

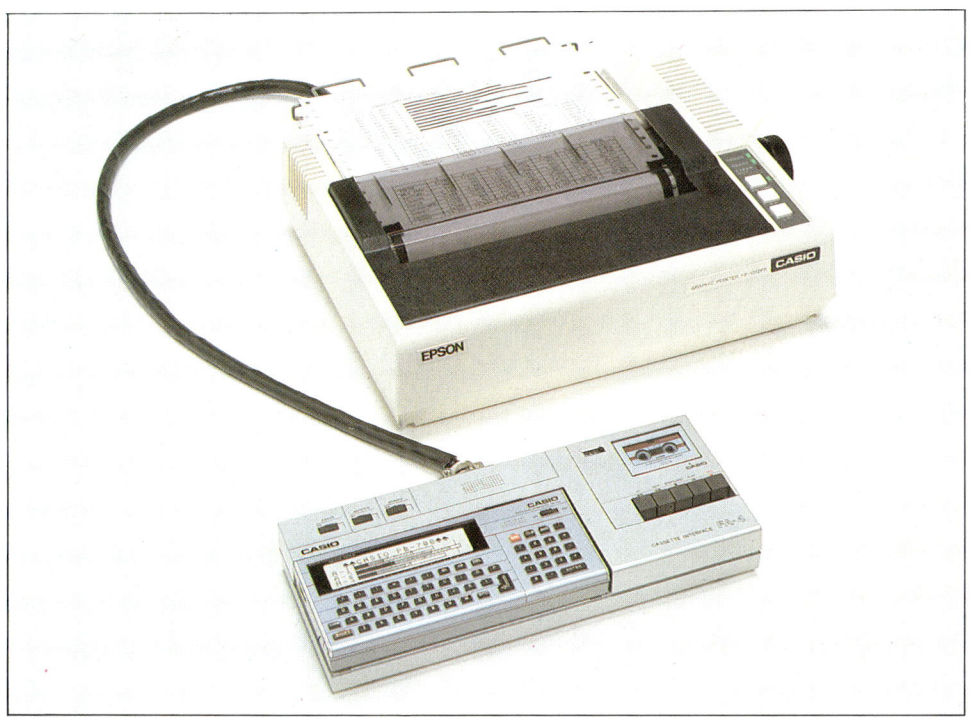

A pocket computer has been turned into a versatile system by the addition of a cassette recorder unit for input/ output, and a dot-matrix printer The computer has only a small built-in LCD (liquid crystal display) screen, but it can also be linked to a monitor screen.

Mice and Things

When computers first came into use they were very complicated to operate. Over the years their hardware and software have been greatly simplified so that now virtually anyone can use them. We say that they have become 'user friendly'. One of the latest developments in user friendliness has been the 'mouse'. This was pioneered by the Apple computer company of the USA on their Lisa model, but it is now also available on the Apple Macintosh and other machines.

The mouse in action

The mouse is a small rolling box attached by wire to the computer. By moving the mouse round the desktop, you automatically move a pointer round the computer screen. The screen is itself designed to look rather like an office desk area. Around the side it has pictures of familiar objects you would find in an office, such as filing cabinet, clipboard, calculator, clock and even a wastepaper basket!

To select the object or function you want, you move the mouse until the pointer points to the appropriate picture. Then you press the button on the mouse, and information about that function appears on the screen. Again, this is usually presented in the form of pictures or symbols for you to select with the mouse. In this way you avoid a lot of preliminary keyboard work and you don't have to memorize all the different programming commands.

The screen of a Macintosh computer during the preparation of a brochure. On the left is a pictorial file of 'tools' and techniques you can use. Using the mouse, you can move the pointer to whichever facility you want, and press the button. (At present the pointer is on 'Cut'.)

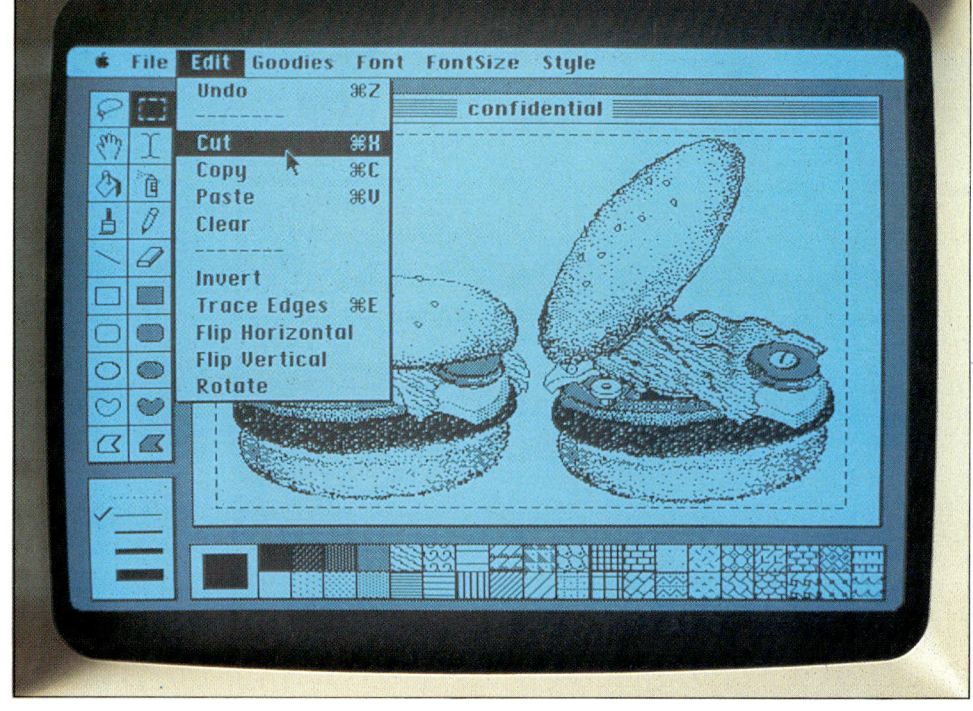

Responding to touch or sound

Some computers have gone one better than the mouse. You can select the various computer functions simply by touching the screen. Also, it will soon be possible to control computers by voice. This is already happening in a small way. The problem is that everyone has a different voice and pronounces words differently, and the computer must have a very large memory to cope with all this information. Currently, computers with a so-called 'speech command' system can handle no more than about 100 words or short phrases.

Some computers can be programmed to answer back! They have a special speech synthesizer chip. This stores sounds, which are then strung together to make words. Because the sounds in speech are complicated, talking computers at present have a limited vocabulary.

British Telecom's City Business System incorporates computer display units with touch-sensitive screens.

Some computers can be commanded by voice rather than by a keyboard. This computer can respond to 50 phrases. But it only responds to the person who programmed it, because it can only recognize their distinctive voice patterns.

Pixels and Graphics

Normally when you operate a computer, letters, figures and symbols appear on the screen. If you look at them carefully you can see that each 'character' is made up of tiny squares. These squares are called picture elements, or pixels. The whole area of the screen is in fact invisibly divided up into squares of pixels. Different combinations or pixels are lit up to form characters when keys on the keyboard are pressed.

A typical home computer might have a VDU screen divided up into 320 pixels horizontally and 256 vertically. This makes nearly 82,000 pixels in all. Typically, it takes a block eight pixels square to form a character. So on the 320 by 256 screen you would be able to write 40 characters (320/8) in each line and 32 lines (256/8) down.

Creating pictures with a computer
The same system of pixels is also used to form pictures on the screen. Such pictures are known as graphics. On most computers you can light up the pixels in any one of up to 16 different colours to give highly coloured graphics. Lighting up each one of the tens of thousands of pixels separately would require a huge memory. So usually the pixels are lit up in groups. The smaller the groups, the better the quality – the higher resolution – of the picture.

The usual way of producing graphics is to instruct the computer

Graphics on a computer are produced by lighting up different pixels in different colours. A face like this is easy to produce, using simple lines.

Letters and figures are also made up of combinations of pixels, as you can see below.

On some computers each pixel can be coloured in any one of hundreds of different colours.

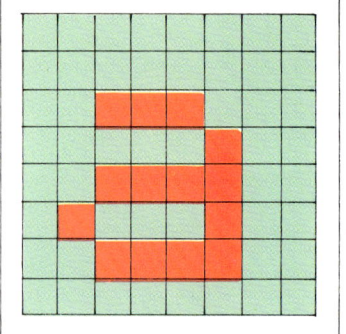

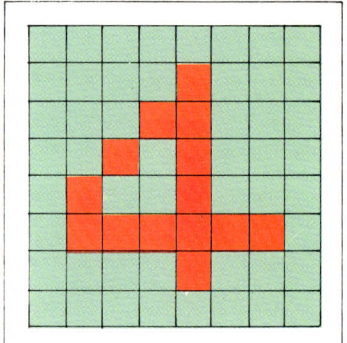

via the keyboard to display certain pixels in certain colours. You identify each pixel by coordinates, usually giving the distance from the left and bottom of the screen. But many computer manufacturers produce special software to help you produce graphics more easily.

Other equipment enables you to draw your own pictures on the screen. One is the graphics pad, or digitizing tablet. You draw on the pad with a pen-like probe and signals go from the pad to the computer, which lights up the appropriate pixels on the screen. In another system you draw on the screen by touching it with a light pen. The pen senses the light the screen gives out and sends signals to the computer to light up the pixels where you have drawn.

Special graphics software is also available to business computer users. It enables them to display, say, sales figures and other statistics in a way that can be more readily understood. These graphics typically take the form of graphs, bar charts, pie charts and maps.

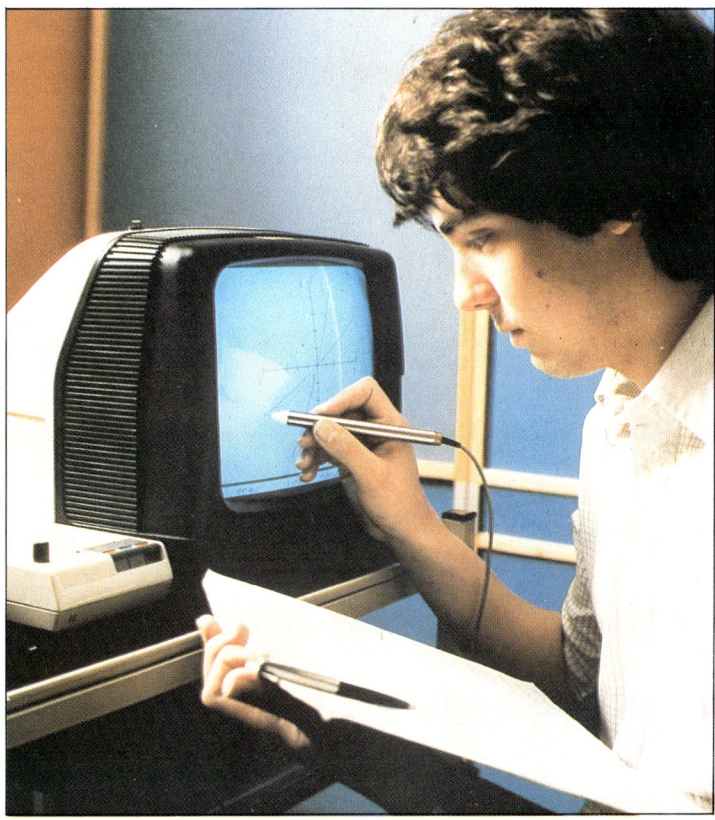

A student uses a light pen to draw on to the computer screen. His computer is linked by telephone lines to that of his tutor, and the drawing appears on the tutor's screen for checking.

Using suitable software and a graphics printer, statistics produced by the computer can be presented in a variety of ways.

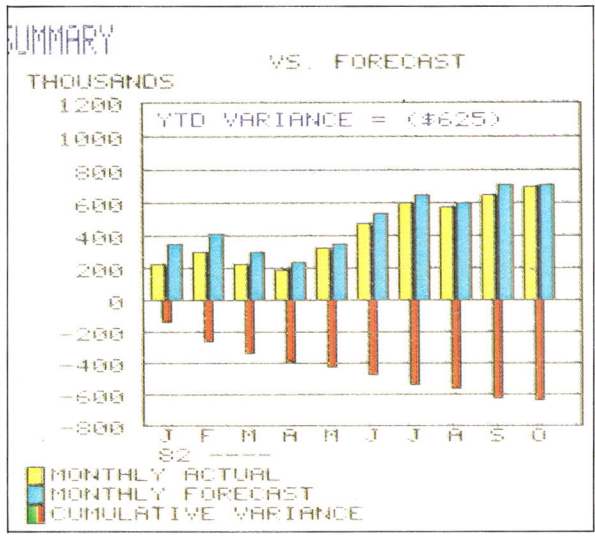

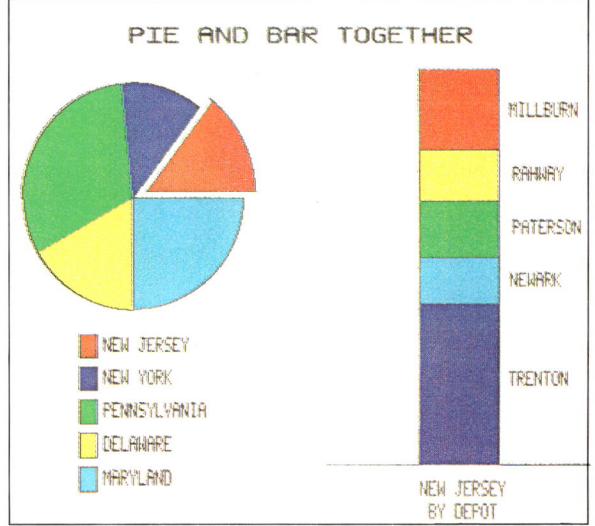

Processing Words

In offices, the most important machine has long been the typewriter, used for writing letters, reports and so on. Thanks again to the silicon chip, the typewriter has become electronic and much more versatile.

The latest electronic typewriters have memories that can store often repeated phrases such as 'Dear Sir' and 'Yours faithfully'. They may also be able to remember and display on a small screen one or more of the previously typed lines so that you can modify, or edit, them.

Chip technology has also brought about great simplification in typewriter design. Even modern electric 'golf-ball' typewriters may have as many as 2500 moving parts. An electronic typewriter may have as few as 100! The greatest simplification has been brought about by incorporating the type characters on the flexible stalks of a plastic 'daisy wheel' a few centimetres across. Conventional typewriters have the type characters at the ends of long pivoted metal levers.

Word-processing hardware and software
From an advanced electronic typewriter it is not a big step to a word processor. This is a purpose-built computer system consisting of keyboard, VDU and printer. It not only acts as a super typewriter, but also carries out many other office tasks, in particular the filing of letters, documents and other information. The filing of course is electronic, data being stored on floppy disks or on tapes.

On a word processor you type out letters or any other text on the keyboard and it appears on the screen. You can alter your text or replace it as you want. It then goes into the machine's memory, so you can retrieve it and edit it any time you like, or change its position on the page or the typeface. Finally, when you are satisfied with the text, you can instruct the printer to print it. It will then be typed out perfectly, with no messy crossings out or overtypings. For most word processors you can get special software that acts like an electronic dictionary. It checks your spelling as you type and corrects any mistakes.

Most purpose-built word processors are used in business. But you can buy word-processing software for most home computers. To print out your text you will of course need a printer, or a compatible electronic typewriter with a suitable connection, or interface, that can take the output signals from the computer.

Like many other advanced microcomputers, the Apple Macintosh has an extensive word-processing program. This is described in the screen display shown here. Using the 'mouse', the user finds his way through the program by moving the pointer (on 'Change' here) to the particular function he requires.

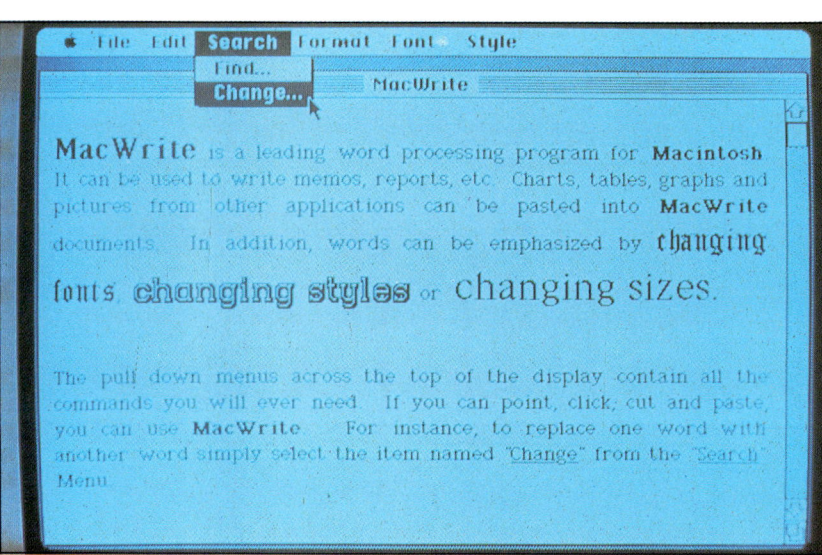

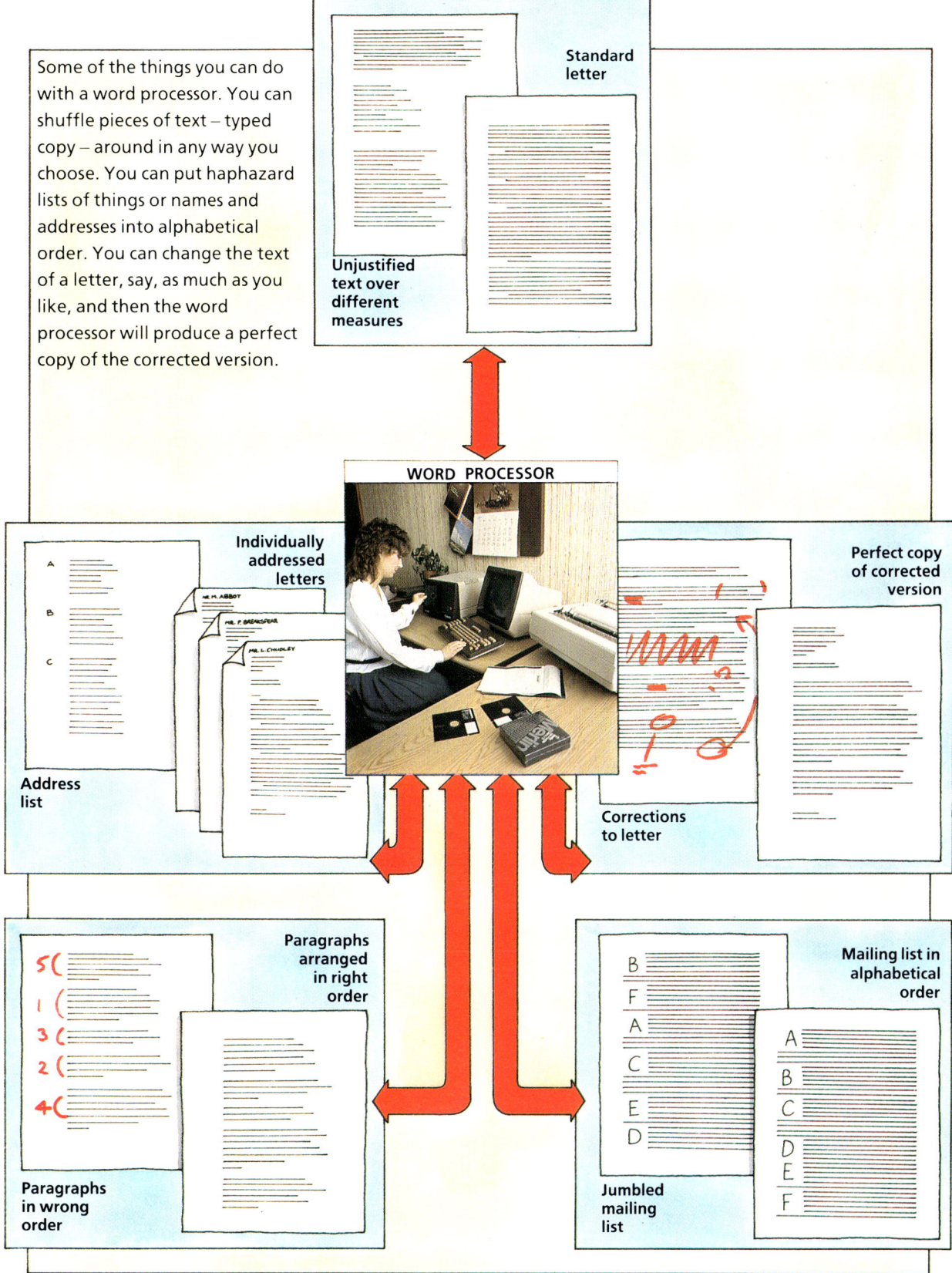

Some of the things you can do with a word processor. You can shuffle pieces of text – typed copy – around in any way you choose. You can put haphazard lists of things or names and addresses into alphabetical order. You can change the text of a letter, say, as much as you like, and then the word processor will produce a perfect copy of the corrected version.

Standard letter

Unjustified text over different measures

WORD PROCESSOR

Individually addressed letters

Address list

Perfect copy of corrected version

Corrections to letter

Paragraphs arranged in right order

Paragraphs in wrong order

Mailing list in alphabetical order

Jumbled mailing list

Networks and Databases

In many offices business people routinely make use of computer technology. They have terminals on their desks that are linked to one another and to a central computer memory bank, which may be located in the same building or elsewhere. The machine illustrated here provides voice as well as data links.

These days, word processors are finding their way into most offices, as business people seek to streamline and speed up their routine work. The larger the business, the more word processors will be required. It would obviously be an advantage if the machines could be linked together so that they could communicate, or talk, with one another. Then people at different computer terminals could exchange information without writing each other letters and memos on paper . Also it would be useful if the word processors could share a high-speed printer and have access to a computer memory larger than their own in-built one.

Such interlinking of equipment and sharing of facilities exists already and is known as a local area network (LAN). Many manufacturers are now designing their word processors and computers so that they can be interlinked. They become work stations within the network. Until recently, machines from different manufacturers were 'incompatible' – they could not usually talk with one another. But some manufacturers are now including in their equipment a standardized communications system that allows this two-way link up.

Modems and viewdata systems

A local area network can readily be expanded to communicate with networks in other locations. This can easily be done over the telephone, using what is called a modem. A modem is a device that changes the output from a computer into signals that can be transmitted along the telephone lines or vice versa. A common type changes the output into sounds that are fed into the telephone mouthpiece. A modem at the receiving end converts the sounds into computer input signals.

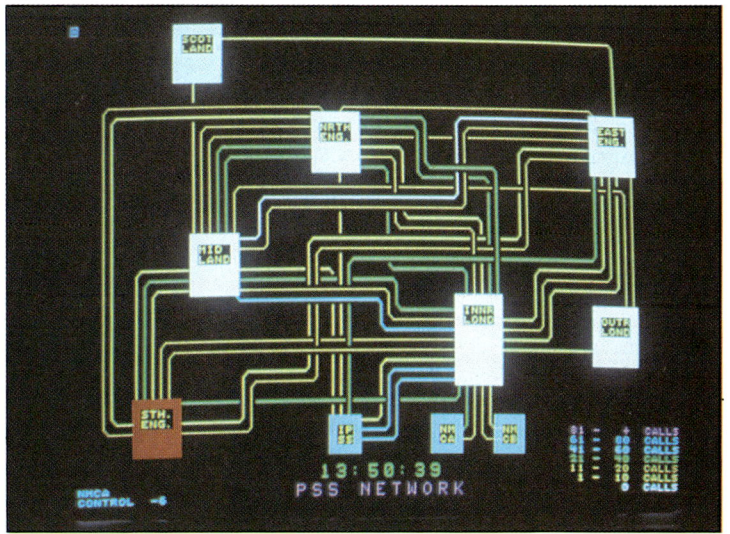

This screen photograph shows a computer data transmission network used by British Telecom in Britain. The data is sent in the form of small 'packets', which may reach their destination by different routes. The technique is called packet switching.

Left: A type of modem for transmitting computer data.

Modems are now widely used by many computer users also to tap into specialist data stored at distant computer centres. These stores are known as databases, or databanks. In the United States there are over 1500 database networks available, for a fee, to computer users. In Britain, computer users can gain access to numerous databases through Prestel. This is the 'viewdata' system provided by British Telecom. In the system, information stored in a powerful central computer is called up, or accessed, over the ordinary telephone lines and is normally displayed on the home television screen. Prestel also allows, through a link-up facility called Gateway, access to other databases run by large companies and organizations.

Viewdata

One of the most extensive computer networks is formed by viewdata systems such as Prestel. It uses telephone links to channel data from a central computer into homes, offices, shops, business organizations, hospitals and so on. The data may be displayed on modified TV sets or on terminals.

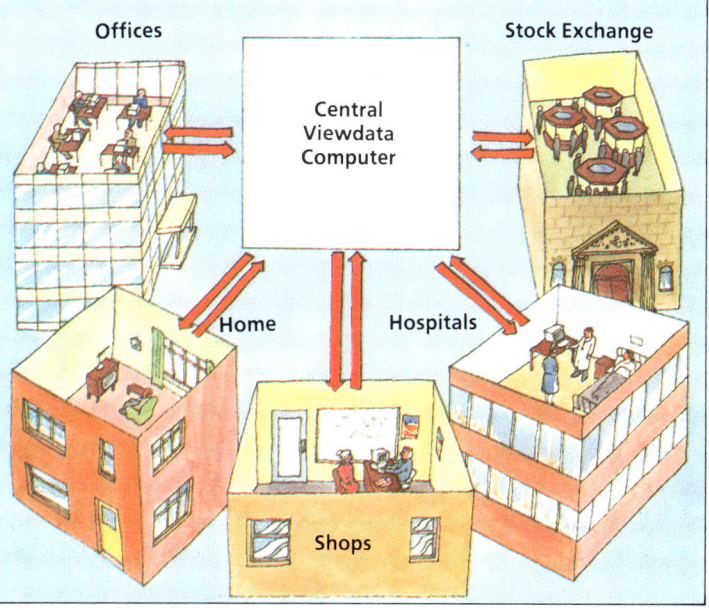

Computers all Around

In the kitchen, in the lounge, in the car and in the shops you cannot escape from the computer or the microchip. Many domestic appliances now incorporate a microchip for control. Automatic washing machines often use a microchip for programming the wash cycles. Electronic sewing machines also are chip-controlled.

For home entertainment, hundreds of electronic games are available both for the home computer and separately. For computer games such as Space Invaders and Pacman you will want to move things around the screen. To play these games you will find a joystick useful. This enables you to move the spaceship, aircraft or whatever around the screen quickly and easily. It may also have a 'fire' button for firing missiles.

Chess enthusiasts may be able to get suitable software for their home computer, or buy a special chess-playing computer such as the Phantom. You can play chess with the Phantom at any one of 12 levels of skill. The computer's pieces move automatically after you have moved. At whatever level you choose to play the Phantom, you will find it hard to beat.

On the move, and in banks and shops

Microchip technology has helped the car to become more efficient by precisely controlling the working of the engine. Some cars now have on-board computers that at the touch of a button can display digitally all kinds of useful information such as fuel consumption and average speed.

In the bank, computers handle all

Top: In the home, computers are widely used to play games, but they are also useful for household accounting, filing and word processing.

Left: Microchips control this car dashboard display and other car systems.

the transactions and prepare your statements. Information printed on your cheques is automatically fed into the bank's computer by a cheque reader. This information is printed at the bottom of the cheque in magnetic ink, and the reader can recognize the magnetic patterns formed by the printed characters. This technique is known as magnetic ink character recognition.

At the supermarket, optical readers are sometimes used at the tills to read the bar code on items purchased. The reader feeds the information to a computer, which tells the till what prices to charge. The computer also notes on a stock list the items that have been sold, and indicates when these items need re-ordering. This is an example of computerized stock control, which is now widespread.

Some banks and offices use optical character recognition (OCR) devices. These detect printed characters and distinguish one from another by their shape. A typed document can be converted directly into computer-code form.

Top: Most high-street banks now have automatic 'Cashpoint' facilities to enable people to obtain money after banking hours. The terminals are linked to the bank's central computer, which checks each customer's account before issuing any money.

Above: This advanced electronic musical instrument (and radio and cassette player) contains special sound synthesizer chips.

Left: A bar-code reader at a supermarket checkout counter. The black-and-white banded bar code is passed over a window and is 'read' by a low-powered laser beam.

Computers in Technology

Computers can help the scientist and technologist in a variety of different ways. Much of their work concerns collecting and recording experimental data from instruments and working out, storing and analysing results. Computers are good at performing these tasks, and they can present the results readily in tabular or graphical form. They can also, from the results, make predictions about what would happen if certain aspects of an experiment were changed.

We are all familiar with the predictions made by the computers the weather men use as these form the basis of our weather forecasts. Only a computer could analyse quickly the volumes of data coming continuously from weather stations and satellites around the world and spot precisely how the weather is developing. It then projects these developments forwards in time and makes a prediction. Many TV weather forecasts show computer-predicted sequences of cloud cover for the day ahead.

False-colour imagery and CAD

Scientists often find colour computer graphics useful for the analysis and presentation of results. And they can extend this technique to the presentation and analysis of photographs and images of things, such as land-survey satellite (Landsat) images of the Earth. The electronic data coming from Landsat can readily be modified by computer to form pictures in colours that are false – not true to life. Such false-colour pictures can reveal a wealth of detail that ordinary photographs of the same areas would miss.

Many designers of equipment, vehicles and structures find the computer invaluable. When suitably programmed, the computer can show a variety of possible designs not only as one flat picture, but in a series of three-dimensional views from different angles. This is known as computer-aided design or CAD for short.

Computers can easily create false-colour imagery showing the heat loss from a house (top) and details in a galaxy.

The doctor's ally

Many high-technology machines could not have been created without the computer. One notable example is the X-ray scanner. This works by what is called computerized tomography. A thin beam of X-rays is used to examine a thin slice of the body from different angles. A computer coupled to X-ray detectors analyses the X-rays scattered by the soft body tissues and builds up a picture of them. Ordinary X-ray techniques cannot show up detail in soft tissues, only bones and teeth. X-ray scanners have proved invaluable for showing up the structure of the brain and detecting brain damage.

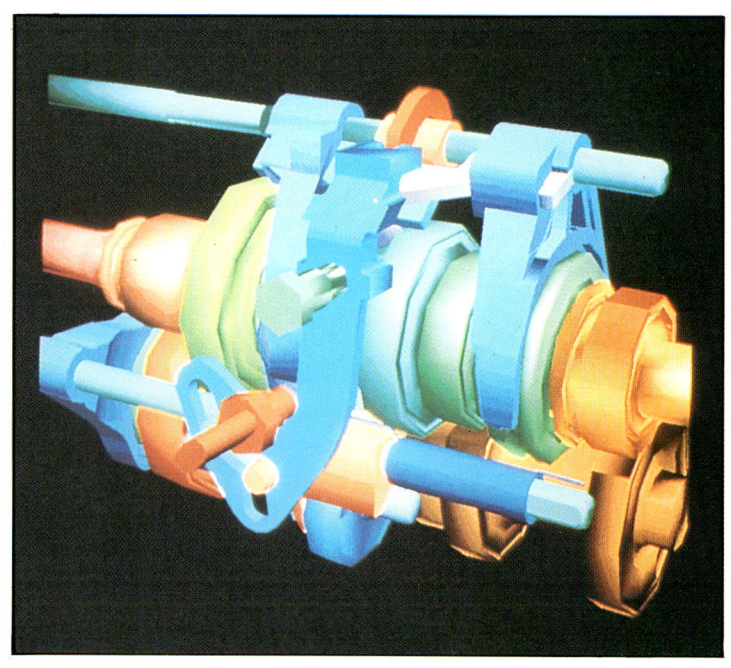

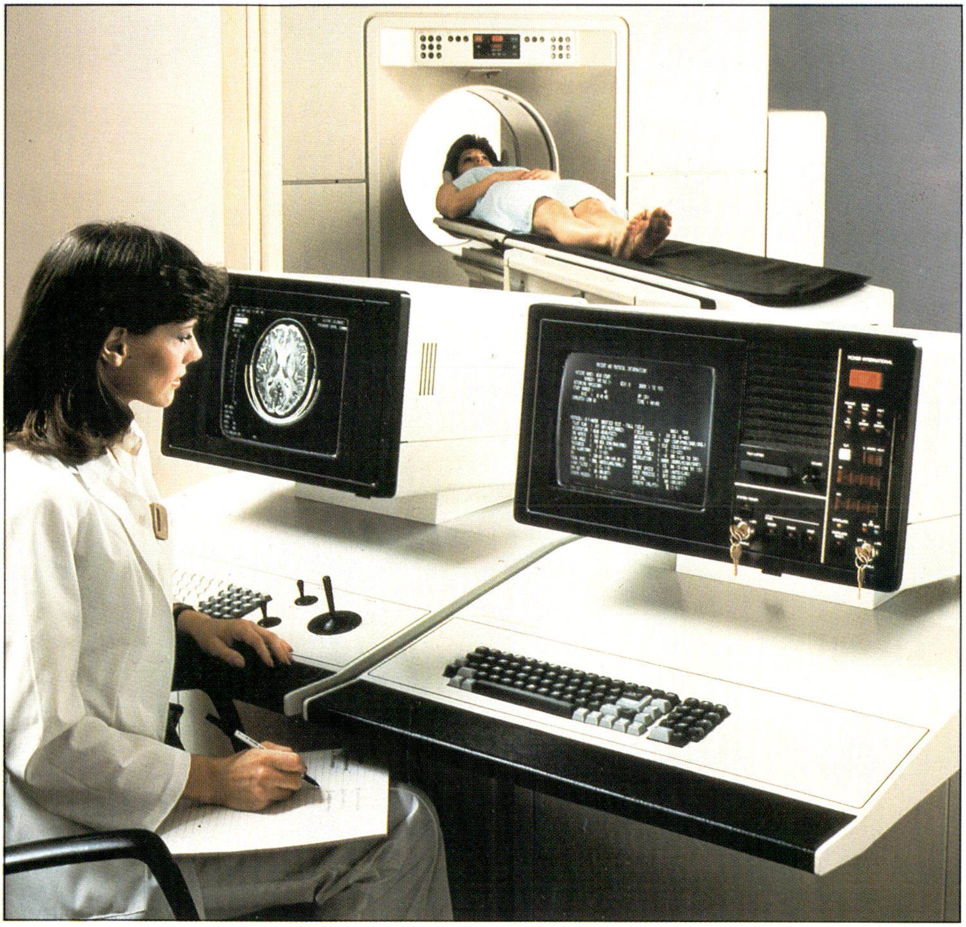

The design for a car gearbox, created with the help of a computer. Computer-aided design is now common in industry. Using computers, various designs can be created and visualized.

An X-ray scanner at work. The patient has her head in the scanning section. Mild X-rays are passed through it from different angles. The results are gathered by computer and displayed as a picture on a screen (left) in front of the operator.

Computers in Control

A modern oil refinery is a huge place, with tall distillation towers, storage tanks, valves and many kilometres of pipelines. Yet it only requires a few workers to run it. This is because it is almost entirely under computer control. The computer is programmed to keep the plant running under ideal conditions of temperature, pressure and so on. It is linked to sensors such as thermometers and pressure gauges in the various vessels and pipes. If the sensors start to register low or high readings, the computer takes action to bring the situation back to normal. If the temperature falls, the computer switches on a heater in the appropriate place. If the pressure falls, it switches on a pump.

This kind of automatic control is an example of what is called automation. Automation is now spreading throughout industry as more and more machines come into use that can control themselves. Many machine tools are like this. A computer feeds instructions to them and checks that the work they produce is as accurate as it should be. It automatically adjusts the equipment as necessary to maintain this accuracy.

Right: An oil refinery at Lavera, France, under computer control. Top right: The control room of a production platform in the North Sea oilfields.

Computerized transport

Automatic control is practised in many transport networks, such as the railways. Part of the London Underground system for example, is under computer control. But perhaps the best example is the Shinkansen, the high-speed railway network of Japan, on which the famous 'bullet trains' run at speeds of over 200 kilometres an hour. The whole 1800 kilometres of route are controlled from a central location.

The most advanced form of computerized transport is the space shuttle. This could not work without powerful computers on the ground at launch and mission controls and on board the shuttle orbiter. The orbiter is such a complicated machine that it can only be flown by computer. During take-off as many as 300,000 operations have to be carried out *every second* to fly the craft. No human being could cope with such a work load.

Three computer video display screens on the instrument console of the space shuttle mission simulator.

A computer-controlled aircraft simulator. The cockpit can be rotated in all directions to mimic real-life flying.

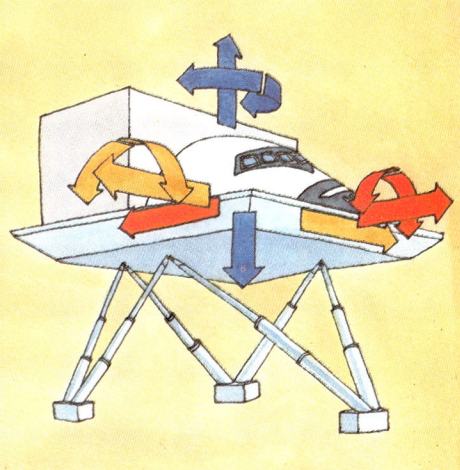

Robots

Quite often these days we see headlines in the newspapers like 'Robots take over'. But do not worry, our world is not being overrun by mechanical people! The robots referred to are computer-controlled machines that can do the kinds of things human beings do. More and more of these robots are now coming into use in factories throughout the world. They are widely used on car assembly lines, usually for welding parts of the car body together.

Industrial robots look nothing like the popular image of a robot – a human-like mechanism with head, arms and legs. This kind of robot is called an android. Some people have built androids for fun, but they have limited uses. Human beings are very complicated things to imitate!

Robots in action

A typical industrial robot has a single arm that can move up and down and in and out. It can swivel round on a pivot. At the end it has flexible joints and a gripper device, which imitate the human wrist and hand. The robot's 'muscles' may work electrically, hydraulically (by liquid pressure) or pneumatically

Large-scale car manufacturers use robots for welding.

Inset: A multiple-exposure photograph of a robot laser cutting torch at work.

(by air pressure). The robot is controlled by a built-in computer.

Before the robot can take its place in the production line, it has to be taught what to do by a human worker. The 'teacher' guides the robot arm through the precise motions it must carry out, and the robot memorizes the movements. Thereafter it can work by itself, drawing on the information in its memory.

The future for robots

Because of microchip technology, computers are now small enough to be fitted into practically any machine that needs controlling. So robot control is bound to increase enormously in the years to come. Because of the extraordinary memory capacity of modern computers, there is virtually no limit on the potential uses of robots. The next generation of machines will be a lot smarter than the present ones. They will be equipped with electronic eyes and more sensitive gripper fingers. Then they will be able to carry out assembly work of many kinds, even of delicate equipment.

Although robots will never be as versatile as human beings, they have many advantages. They can work accurately for long periods, doing repetitive work that would bore and tire human workers. They can also work in noise, glare, fumes and other dangerous environments that humans would find intolerable.

This floor robot is appropriately called a turtle. It can be programmed to draw simple geometric designs. Floor robots are often used in schools to explore computer control systems.

George, a toy robot. Most toy robots can be programmed via a calculator-type keyboard to perform a number of routine moves, repeat a series of calculations, or to play a tune.

Milestones

2000s BC
The abacus comes into use in early civilizations. It is still widely used today in the Far East for everyday calculations. It generally takes the form of sets of beads strung on wires within a wooden frame.

AD 1617
The Scottish mathematician John Napier, who invented logarithms, devises a method of multiplying and dividing using rods or 'bones' printed with the multiplication tables.

1622
The English mathematician William Oughtred builds a slide rule for making calculations, again using logarithms to mark out the scales.

1642
The French mathematician-philosopher Blaise Pascal builds a mechanical calculating machine, the forerunner of the desk calculating machines used widely until a few years ago. It consists of a train of number wheels and a gear system for 'carrying'.

1671
The German mathematician Gottfried Leibnitz invents a calculating machine called the 'Stepped Reckoner', which can multiply and divide and take square roots, as well as add and subtract. In 1679 he develops the binary number system with which modern computers operate.

1835
The English inventor Charles Babbage begins work on a machine called the Analytical Engine, which can be seen as the earliest direct ancestor of the modern computer. It has a method of programming, using punched cards, and a memory for storing data. Babbage prepares detailed drawings of the Engine, but it is never built.

1886
Herman Hollerith in the United States begins work on a tabulating machine in which data is fed in on punched cards. The cards are read electrically by the machine.

1911
Hollerith joins with two other companies to form the Computing Tabulating Recording Company, which later becomes the famous International Business Machines (IBM).

1944
Howard H. Aiken, working with IBM, completes the first digital computer at Harvard University, called the Mark 1 or Automatic Sequence Controlled Calculator. Calculations are controlled by electromechanical switches.

1945
The first all-electronic computer is completed at the University of Pennsylvania. Called the Electronic Numerical Integrator and Calculator (ENIAC), it contains over 18,000 valves.

1947
John von Neumann in the United States designs a computer which can store programs, coded numerically.

1950
The first mass-produced computer goes on sale, the Univac (Universal Automatic Computer), built in Philadelphia.

1950-1960
Transistors are used in computers, greatly reducing their size and cost.

1958
Texas Instruments in the United States produces the first integrated circuit, further reducing the size of electronic circuits and leading to the development of the modern silicon chip.

1964
IBM produces the first word processor, by modifying an electric typewriter.

1971
Intel Corporation in the United States develops the microprocessor, which contains all the computing functions of a computer on a single chip, and is appropriately called the 'computer on a chip'. Digital calculators and digital watches come on to the market.

1974
In Britain, the Post Office (the part now operating as British Telecom) introduces the first viewdata service, called Prestel, in which information from a central computer can be accessed via the telephone lines and displayed on the TV screen.

1980
Sinclair in Britain launches a personal computer, the ZX-80, for under £100.

Glossary

automation	The widespread use of automatic machines in industry, controlled by computer.
bar code	A code of thick and thin black bands now printed on most goods, which can be read by computer-controlled equipment.
binary code	The system used to represent numbers for handling by computer. It uses only two digits, 0 and 1, the so-called binary digits or bits.
bit	A binary digit. See **binary code**.
bug	A fault in a program.
chip	A silicon chip.
computer language	A simplified language which programmers use to feed instructions to the computer. The computer itself translates the language into binary machine code, which it can use.
data	The information that a computer handles.
database	A store of information, usually relating to a certain topic.
de-bugging	Looking for and correcting mistakes in a program.
digital computer	The ordinary kind of computer, which handles information and instructions in the form of coded numbers or digits.
doping	Treating a silicon chip with chemical vapours so as to change its electrical properties.
floppy disks	Flexible magnetic disks used to store instructions and information for use in a computer or word processor.
flowchart	A diagram setting out the various steps in a computer program.
graphics	Pictures produced by a computer.
hard copy	Data produced by a computer in the form of figures and words on printed paper.
hardware	The various pieces of equiment that make up a computer system, e.g. VDU, keyboard, printer. Contrast **software**.
input	Any information and instructions fed into a computer.
integrated circuit	An electronic circuit consisting of many different components contained within a single crystal (chip).
interface	An electronic device that changes computer signals into a form that other electronic equipment (such as an electronic typewriter) can use.
LCD	Short for liquid crystal display. The black-on-white display on pocket calculators and digital watches.

machine code	The binary code computers use to represent information and instructions.
mainframe	The most powerful kind of computer, with an extensive memory and rapid computing ability.
memory	The part of a computer that stores information and instructions. See **RAM** and **ROM**.
microchip	Another name for a silicon chip, which contains microscopically small electronic circuits.
microcomputer	The ordinary home computer.
microdrive	A miniature tape unit used for input/output on some computers. The tape is wound inside a tiny cartridge.
minicomputer	A computer that is one step up from the microcomputer and has a larger memory and faster computing capability.
output	Information that comes out of the computer.
modem	A device that converts computer signals into a form that can be transmitted over the telephone lines, and vice versa. It is short for modulator/de-modulator.
mouse	A rolling ball device used as a pointer or cursor with some computers.
peripherals	Additional equipment that you can connect to a computer, such as plotters and printers.
pixels	Short for picture cells (elements); small squares on the computer display screen which can be lit up to form letters or pictures.
program	A step-by-step set of instructions that tells the computer what to do.
RAM	Short for random access memory. The computer memory that stores information, instructions and results relating to the particular work being done at any time. The memory is erased after the computer is switched off.
ROM	Short for read only memory. The computer memory that stores the instructions that tell it how to work. It is a permanent memory.
silicon chip	A thin wafer of silicon, a few millimetres square, which contains miniaturized electronic circuits, made up typically of thousands upon thousands of separate components.
software	The program or set of instructions that is fed into a computer. Contrast **hardware**.
synthesizer	A device in a computer that produces sounds.
VDU	Short for visual display unit. The TV-type screen on which information and instructions for the computer are displayed.
word processor	A computer-based unit which you can use to write and edit letters and other text, file them, and so on. Word-processing software is now available for many general computers.

Index

Acknowledgements

The editor would like to extend his grateful thanks to the many organizations and individuals who provided information and pictures for the book. He is particularly indebted to Neil Johannessen of Telecom Technology Showcase, Jane Marrow and Steve Lewington of TeleFocus at British Telecom Centre, and Joan Callieu, Kim Fitzsimmons and Sharon Cartwright at British Telecom International Publicity; to Malcolm Smythe, who created the visual presentation of his ideas; to Dee Robinson for the picture research – assisted by Francesca Wolf; and to Vivienne Canter who helped him develop the series idea when at Telecom Technology Showcase.

The designer would like to thank Graham Baylis at Dorchester Typesetting.

The Dataworld series of books was produced with the assistance of the Telecom Technology Showcase, British Telecom's exhibition, resource and information centre. Through a unique series of displays, videos and working models, Telecom Technology Showcase brings alive over 200 years of telecommunications history as well as offering a glimpse of the future of information technology.

Telecom Technology Showcase,
135 Queen Victoria Street,
London EC4V 4AT.
Telephone: 01-248 7444
Open Monday - Friday 10.00 – 17.00
Admission Free

PICTURE CREDITS
(T=top, B=Bottom, C=centre, L=left, R=right)
8-9 AT&T Bell Laboratories   10T Thorn EMI Ferguson   10B Sinclair Research
11 Motorola Inc.   12 TeleFocus/British Telecom   13T IBM   13BL TeleFocus/British Telecom   13BR TeleFocus/British Telecom
14BL Casio Electronics   14BR Seiko
15 AT&T Bell Laboratories   16T Casio Electronics   16C Sinclair Research
16B ICL Computers   18BL and 18BR Ferranti
21 Research Machines   22 Apple Computers   23T Sinclair Research   23B Casio Electronics   24 Apple Computers
25T TeleFocus/British Telecom   25B Texas Instruments   26 Computer Games Ltd.
27T TeleFocus/British Telecom
27BL & 27R Computer Pictures Ltd.   28 Apple Computers   30 GEC   31T & 31C TeleFocus/British Telecom   32T IBM
32B Motorola Inc.   33T IBM   33C Casio Electronics   33B IBM   34 Pat Wallace/ Rutherford Appleton Lab. (galaxy): AGEMA Infrared Systems (house)   35T IBM
35B Picker International   36 & 37T British Petroleum   37B NASA   38 ASEA (car robot); Culham Laboratory (laser cutter)
39T Computer Games Ltd.   39B Jessop Electronics.
Cover photo: Paul Brierley